A Horn for Louis

A Horn for Louis

by Eric A. Kimmel • illustrated by James Bernardin

A STEPPING STONE BOOK™

Random House New York

Text copyright © 2005 by Eric A. Kimmel.
Illustrations copyright © 2005 by James Bernardin.
All rights reserved under International and Pan-American Copyright Conventions.
Published in the United States by Random House Children's Books,
a division of Random House, Inc., New York, and simultaneously in Canada
by Random House of Canada Limited, Toronto.

www.steppingstonesbooks.com
www.randomhouse.com/kids

Library of Congress Cataloging-in-Publication Data
Kimmel, Eric A.
A horn for Louis / Eric Kimmel.
p.   cm.
"A Stepping Stone book."
ISBN 0-375-83252-1 (trade) — ISBN 0-375-93252-6 (lib. bdg.)
1. Armstrong, Louis, 1901–1971—Juvenile literature.
2. Jazz musicians—United States—Biography—Juvenile literature.
I. Title.   ML3930.A75K56 2005   781.65'092—dc22   2005004151

Printed in the United States of America   First Edition   10 9 8 7 6 5 4 3 2 1

RANDOM HOUSE and colophon are registered trademarks and A STEPPING STONE BOOK and
colophon are trademarks of Random House, Inc.

To the people of New Orleans

Contents

1

A New Orleans Morning

Louis rubbed his eyes. The room was dark and cold. Louis wanted to sleep some more, but it was time to get up. Louis had to go to work.

Louis always tried not to move around too much when he got up. He did not want to wake his mother or his little sister.

Louis didn't have a bedroom of his own. He didn't even have a real bed. Louis lived in a shack off a run-down street called Brick Row. His bed was a pile of quilts spread on the floor. He shared them with his mother, May Ann, and his little sister, Mama Lucy. Sharing a bed with two other people was a good way to keep warm on cold winter nights. But there was no good way to stay warm when it was time to get up.

Louis gave his sleeping sister a kiss. "Be sweet, Mama Lucy. I'll see you tonight."

Mama Lucy's real name was Beatrice, but nobody ever called her that. Everyone knew her as Mama Lucy, even though she was only five years old. Just about everybody on Brick Row had a nickname: Boat Nose, Rhythm Jaws, Hammock Face. Louis had a nickname, too. Most of his friends called him Dipper. That was short for "Dipper Mouth." Louis loved to laugh. When he did, he opened his mouth so wide it looked like the bowl of the dipper in the courtyard water barrel.

Louis took a deep breath and rolled out from under the quilts. Ooooh! Was it cold! Louis hopped around in the dark. He shivered as he tried to find his clothes. He slept in his long johns, so he didn't have to look for them. His mother, May Ann, had ironed a clean shirt for him and left it on a chair. Louis pulled the shirt over his head. He buttoned it up all the way to the collar.

Stockings came next. Then knee pants. Man, there sure were a lot of buttons! Knee buttons and fly buttons and suspender buttons. Getting all the buttons in the right buttonholes was hard enough. Doing it in the dark when the cold made your fingers stiff was even harder.

Louis finally got his clothes buttoned. He slipped his suspenders over his shoulders. Now for his shoes.

Even shoes had buttons. Louis used a buttonhook to pull the shoe buttons through the holes.

"The man who invented shoe buttons should be run out of town," Louis grumbled.

He kept his voice low so he wouldn't wake May Ann or Mama Lucy.

One day, Louis would find a way to make lots of money. Then they'd live in a big house with their own bedrooms and their own beds. *It would be nice to have a bed of my own,* Louis thought. A real bed in his own room. It would have fluffy pillows and clean white sheets.

Louis's grandmother told him about beds like that. She used to work in the big houses in the Garden District. She cooked and cleaned for rich white people. The beds in those houses were so big and soft! Sleeping there must be like sleeping on a cloud.

"I'll have a bed like that, and a house like that someday," Louis promised himself. "I'll keep the fire in the stove going all night long so it will be warm in the morning. I'll have servants to button my buttons and light the kerosene lamp so I won't ever have to get dressed in the dark. Why, I may not even need those lamps! I'll sleep so late that when I wake up, it'll be time to go back to bed!"

It sure was a fine dream. Although Louis was only seven years old, he was already trying to make it come true.

Louis worked at the Karnofsky junkyard. He made a dollar a day. One dollar was a lot of money for Louis's family. It bought food to eat. It bought coal for the stove. Louis's mother worked at a place where they baled up old newspapers. They only paid her fifty cents a day!

Louis felt proud that he could help his family. Christmas was only two weeks away. Louis hoped that he could earn extra money to buy presents for his mother and sister. Maybe he would have enough money to buy something special for himself.

"Louis, why didn't you wake me up? I'll make some lunch for you." Louis heard his mother getting out from under the quilts.

"No, Mama. Go back to sleep," Louis whispered. "You can make something for Mama Lucy when she wakes up. You don't need to go to any trouble for me. Mama Karnofsky likes to cook. She gets worried if I don't eat enough."

"Are you sure, Louis?" his mother asked. "Those people you work for must be awfully kind to take care of you the way they do. I worry that they do too much. We work hard and we get by. We may not have much money, but we always pay our own way."

"I know that, Mama," said Louis. "I told you, you can't argue with Mama Karnofsky. I just eat what she puts on my plate. That makes her happy."

It made Louis happy, too. The food that Mama Karnofsky put on Louis's plate was mighty good. Mama Karnofsky loved to cook as much as Louis loved to eat. She made *lokshen* and *knaidlach* and dishes whose names Louis couldn't begin to pronounce. That didn't matter to Louis. He might not be able to say them, but he sure could eat them!

Louis's mother kissed him goodbye. "Be sweet, son. Work hard and be a good boy."

"You know I will, Mama. You can count on me," Louis said as he pulled on his jacket. He slipped his tin horn into his pocket. Shutting the door behind him, he walked through the alley.

Louis heard music. The music came from Perdido Street, the main street of Storyville. Everybody in New Orleans knew about the part of town called Storyville. People in Storyville loved to have a good time. They danced. They sang. They played music. In Storyville, fun and music never stopped. Music played day and night. It poured from every door.

The music had many names. Some called it blues. Some called it ragtime. Some called it jazz. Louis didn't care what they called it. He loved it all. The music made his feet dance. He marched along the pavement and pretended he was leading a big parade. He was the Grand Marshal.

A horn began to play. Louis shivered. Only one person in New Orleans could play like that. Joe Oliver! *King* Oliver!

Louis stopped by Pete Lala's place and looked through the open door. He saw Joe Oliver standing up on the little stage, blowing his trumpet. Joe blew low and sad, strong and sweet at the same time. Some said he played like an angel. Some said he played like the devil. Nobody alive could blow horn like Joe Oliver. That was why everybody in Storyville called him King.

Louis took out his tin horn. He put it to his lips. He made believe he was playing, too. Louis felt music rise from his heart. He felt it come to life with each breath. His fingers moved up and down on the toy horn. The toy horn didn't have valves like a real trumpet. Still, Louis liked to pretend that he knew how to use valves to make the notes.

The people inside Pete Lala's started cheering for Joe Oliver. Louis pretended they were cheering for him. "Hooray for King Louis!" they yelled.

If only he had a real horn to play. Not just a little tin toy.

"Ain't never gonna blow like King Oliver on this tin horn," Louis whispered to himself. He put his dream back in his pocket with the tin horn. Louis had to hurry. He did not want to be late for work.

2

The Junkyard

The junkyard where Louis worked stood on the corner of Franklin and Perdido streets. It was just a block from the Girod Street Cemetery. To get to work, Louis had to walk by the cemetery in the dark.

There isn't much high ground in New Orleans. Most of the city is below the level of the Mississippi River, which flows past it. High walls called levees keep the water out. But water is never far away.

Water would quickly fill a grave dug in the

ground. So people in New Orleans are laid to rest aboveground in cement and marble buildings. These buildings make a New Orleans cemetery look like a little town—a city of the dead!

A Horn for Louis

Some of Louis's friends were afraid to walk by the cemetery at night. Not Louis. He figured that the ghosts, if there were any, were on their way home by now.

"G'morning, spooks!" Louis laughed in a loud voice. "Did you all have a good night? Sweet dreams now. Don't let the bedbugs bite."

Then he ran, just in case one of the spooks didn't find that so funny.

Louis ran all the way to the junkyard. He arrived just as the first slice of the sun appeared above the roofs of New Orleans.

The sign above the junkyard gate said, "Karnofsky and Sons. We Buy Paper, Rags, Old Iron."

"Good morning, Alex! Good morning, Morris!" Louis called to the two Karnofsky boys. Alex and Morris were older than Louis. They treated him like a little brother.

Louis helped Alex and Morris harness their horse, Rosie, to the junk wagon. Rosie liked Louis. She lowered her head so Louis could scratch her ears.

"Got your horn?" Alex, the youngest Karnofsky, asked Louis.

"You bet!" said Louis. He took the tin horn from his pocket. It was dented in the middle and the wooden mouthpiece was gone. Louis had to blow through two fingers to get a sound out of it. Louis didn't mind. A tin horn was better than no horn at all. He blew a snappy ragtime tune.

"That's great!" Alex said.

Morris, his older brother, agreed. "King Oliver better watch out," Morris said. "Louis is getting real good on that horn. He'll be the king of New Orleans someday."

"Louis could be better than good," Alex said. "Don't you think he needs a real horn? I wonder how he can get one."

"I wish I knew," Louis said. "Horns cost a lot of money. I don't know how I'd ever save enough to buy a real one."

"You never know," said Alex. "Today could be the day. Go see Mama. She wants to make sure you eat breakfast before we leave."

"I already ate breakfast," Louis said. He didn't want to tell Alex or Morris the truth.

"Then you'll eat another one," said Morris. "We know how much you like to eat. Hurry! It's almost time to go."

* * *

Louis ran to the little house at the end of the junkyard. Pop Karnofsky was reading the newspaper.

"Hello, Pop!" Louis said when he came through the door.

Pop Karnofsky looked up. "Hello, Louis. Are you ready to go to work?" he asked.

"Louis will be ready to go to work after he eats," said Mama Karnofsky. "Louis, go wash your hands."

"Yes, ma'am." Louis carefully washed his hands at the sink. He dried them on the towel. Then he sat down at the table.

Mama Karnofsky filled a bowl with her special grits. She called it *kasha*. She buttered a thick slice of black bread. She filled a glass with milk. "Eat, Louis," she said. "How can you be big and strong if you don't eat?"

Louis didn't argue. Morris was right. He loved to eat. Louis ate two bowls of kasha. He ate three slices of black bread. He drank two glasses of milk. He drank a mug of tea.

Now he was ready to go.

"Tell Alex to come home early," Mama Karnofsky said. "Hanukkah starts tonight."

"What's Hanukkah?" Louis asked.

"It's a holiday. A Jewish holiday," Pop Karnofsky said. He smiled at Louis. "You'll come tonight. You'll learn all about it."

"Thanks for my breakfast, Mama," Louis said. He carried his bowl, glass, and mug to the sink. He heard Alex calling, "Hurry up! Rosie wants to get going!"

"I'm coming!" Louis ran out the door. He jumped into the wagon and sat down beside Alex. Alex flicked the reins. Rosie started walking, *clip-clop, clip-clop,* between the piles of junk that filled the yard. Morris opened the gate to let the wagon through.

Louis thought about what Pop Karnofsky had said. He knew the Karnofskys were Jewish. He just wasn't sure what being Jewish meant. He did know that the Karnofskys were different from most of the other families he knew.

Pop Karnofsky always wore a hat, inside and outside the house.

Mama Karnofsky never cooked ham or pork. She never served milk and meat together.

They closed the junkyard on Saturday, not

Sunday. "It is our Sabbath. We call it *Shabbos*," Alex once explained.

In some ways they were real different. Not many white families would let a black child sit at their table and eat from their dishes. Louis's mother hadn't believed it when he'd told her.

"They must be good people," she'd said.

They are *good people,* Louis thought. He suddenly remembered what he was supposed to tell Alex. "Mama says we have to come home early. Tonight is . . . is . . ." Louis could not remember the word.

"Hanukkah," said Alex. "I didn't forget. Got your horn?"

"Yeah," said Louis.

"Then off we go!" said Alex. "The junk is waiting!"

3

In the Alley

The city was waking up. Louis smelled fresh coffee. He smelled the special New Orleans doughnuts called *beignets*. The market opened and people called out what they had to sell.

"Fresh bread! Bread! Hot from the oven!"

"Watermelon! So sweet and ripe! Fresh watermelon!"

"Tomatoes! Tomatoes! Tomatoes!"

"Banana! Banana!"

"Fish! Catfish! Come and buy!"

Each call was like a song. Louis took out his

tin horn. He made up tunes to go with the calls he heard.

Alex had a call, too. It went, "Rags! Clothes! Bottles! Old iron!"

Louis made up a tune to go with Alex's call. People liked to hear Louis play. They brought their junk to Alex. Alex paid a penny for a big sack of bottles and tin cans. He loaded the junk in the back of the wagon.

"You keep playing. I'll load the junk," Alex told Louis. "Your horn brings the people. They save their junk for us so they can hear you blow your horn. Your horn makes people happy."

"I wish I had a real horn," Louis said. "I'd play like King Oliver. I'd make lots more people happy."

"That day will come," Alex said. "I know it will. For now, you're doing fine. The three of us make a good team. You, me, and Rosie."

"And my horn," said Louis. He started playing faster.

Children came running. Louis saw many of his cousins. He saw many of his friends.

"Play, Louis! Play that horn!" they told him.

The children loved to hear Louis make music. They searched the alleys for cans and bottles. They put them in sacks. They brought them to the wagon. They danced together in the street while Louis played. Some people even tossed pennies to Louis. Alex picked up the pennies and gave them to Louis. "Keep playing," Alex said.

A man came walking along the street with his girlfriend. Louis could tell the man was a "sport." "Sports" were the best-dressed fellows in New Orleans. Most were gamblers. They lived fast and hard. They won or lost hundreds of dollars playing dice or cards.

Lady Luck must be smiling on this dude, Louis thought. The man wore a fine suit and a brand-new hat. His high-button shoes shined as brightly as the diamond ring on his finger and the gold tooth in his mouth. Louis started blowing his tin horn as hard as he could.

"Listen to that boy play!" the sport's girlfriend said. "He has talent."

"Yes, he does!" the sport said. "Too bad he doesn't have a real horn. That tin horn's nothing! It's a piece of junk."

The sport reached into his pocket. He took out a coin and tossed it into the wagon. "Get yourself a real horn!"

Louis picked up the coin. It was a silver dollar!

"Look, Alex," Louis said. "A whole buck! We're doing good! Fifty cents for you and fifty cents for me!"

"No," said Alex. "It's a dollar for you. You earned it. That sport liked the way you blew your horn."

Louis was amazed. Children would toss pennies to hear him play. But a whole dollar! He couldn't believe it.

"If you can make a dollar with that little beat-up tin horn, there's no telling how far you could go with a real one," Alex said.

"Yeah!" said Louis. A horn of his own. A trumpet. Or even a little cornet. How many more dollars would he need?

Alex drove the junk wagon to a part of town called the French Quarter. It was the oldest part of New Orleans, built when the city belonged to France. Some of the houses were so old that they had to lean against each other to keep from falling down. The wagon passed beneath iron balconies that hung over the street.

Many Italian people lived in the Quarter. They loved music.

"Hey, *bambino*! Play your horn for us!"

Louis began to play. People came out on the balconies to listen. Children followed the wagon, dancing in the street. A boy ran up to the wagon. He was older and bigger than Louis.

"How can you make music come out of that little piece of tin?" he asked. "It doesn't even have a mouthpiece."

Louis showed him how he held his fingers

together and blew through them to make a sound. Without warning, the boy snatched the tin horn from Louis's hands.

"Come back with that!" Alex shouted.

Louis jumped from the wagon. "Give me my horn!" he yelled, running after the boy. The big boy laughed and tossed the horn to another boy. Louis ran after him.

"Come and get it!" the boys yelled, tossing the horn back and forth. It was a game for them, but not for Louis. He needed that horn. Alex couldn't help him. He had to stay with the wagon. Louis had to get his horn back by himself.

The boys ran down an alley. Louis ran after them. The alley turned and twisted. Louis could no longer see the boys, but he could hear them laughing. He followed their voices.

The alley opened up into a courtyard filled with trash. Louis saw the boys gathered in the corner. There were seven of them and one of him. They looked tough. Louis couldn't out-fight them. He'd have to outthink them.

The biggest boy was trying to play the tin horn. He couldn't get more than a buzz out of it. Louis walked right up to him.

"You'll never get it to play that way. Do you want me to show you how to do it?" Louis asked.

"Yeah," the boy said. He handed Louis the horn. The other boys gathered around to watch.

Louis ducked between them and ran. The boys chased after him. Louis ran down the alley. Which way should he go? Right? Left? This wasn't his neighborhood. He didn't know these streets. They ran every which way, like a tangled bundle of old wire in the back of the junk wagon. The boys were getting closer. Louis knew he was in big trouble if they caught him.

Suddenly he heard a familiar cry. "Rags!

Clothes! Bottles! Old iron!" It was Alex, calling for him. The junk wagon had to be near.

Louis ran toward Alex's voice. The alley opened up onto a street. There was the junk wagon! Louis leaped into the back among the piles of junk.

The boys stopped in their tracks. Alex stood up, holding the cart whip that he used to guide Rosie. "Do you boys want something?" he asked them.

The boys slunk back into the alley, mumbling to themselves. Alex waited until they were out of sight before turning to Louis.

"Are you crazy?" he asked him. "What's the idea? Those boys belong to a street gang. They could have beat you bloody."

"I got my horn back," Louis said.

"Did you?" said Alex. "Take a look at it."

Louis stared at the squashed tin tube that used to be his horn. He had fallen on it when he jumped into the wagon. When he tried to straighten it out, the horn snapped in two.

"My horn!" Louis screamed.

"The horn is *kaput*. Finished. May it rest in peace," Alex said.

"What am I gonna do?" Louis wailed.

"You'll get a new one," Alex answered. "It's about time. I was getting tired of listening to that old piece of junk."

"How am I gonna pay for a new horn?" Louis demanded to know.

"The sport gave you a dollar. It's a start." Alex grinned. "Let's go shopping."

4

The Pawnshop

Alex stopped the wagon in front of a pawn-shop. It was on the corner of Rampart and Perdido streets. Louis got down from the wagon and walked up to the window. He looked inside.

"Do you see anything you like?" Alex asked.

Louis saw guitars, trombones, and clarinets hanging in the window. He saw saxophones, violins, and banjos. And one trumpet!

The trumpet looked new. Its polished brass shined. Louis stood on tiptoe. He pressed his nose against the window. That trumpet was the most beautiful horn Louis had ever seen. Then he looked at the price tag.

Twenty-five dollars!

Louis's shoulders sagged. He looked at the silver dollar in his hand. That trumpet might as well have been made of gold. It cost a lot more money than he had. It cost more money than he had ever seen in his life!

Louis turned back toward the wagon.

"Where are you going?" Alex asked.

"Back to the junkyard," Louis said. "That horn costs too much money. I couldn't even dream enough money to buy it."

"Don't give up," said Alex. "We just started looking. There must be thousands of horns in New Orleans. Who knows? Maybe we can talk to the pawnshop man. He might be willing to bargain. He might have another horn you can buy. Let's go in and have a look around. Looking around doesn't cost anything."

Louis and Alex tied Rosie's reins to a street lamp. They walked into the pawnshop together.

"We were looking at that trumpet in the

window," Alex said to the man behind the counter. "How much do you want for it?"

"Twenty-five dollars, like the price tag says. It's a real good buy," the man answered. "That horn used to belong to a fellow who played with King Oliver. He fell on hard times and had to sell his horn. Bad luck for him. Good luck for you. Would you like to play it? See how it sounds?"

"Not me!" said Alex. "I can't play the horn. I can't even sing. I couldn't carry a tune if you put it in my wagon. But I'll bet my partner Louis can play any tune you'd like. How about letting him try?"

The man made a sour face. He went to the store's front window and took out the gleaming horn. He replaced the mouthpiece with one he kept on a shelf. Louis and Alex both knew why he did that. White people wouldn't buy a horn that a black person's lips had touched. How well he could play didn't matter.

Louis felt ashamed and so did Alex. But they didn't say anything. They wanted a horn.

Louis lifted the trumpet to his mouth. He pressed the mouthpiece against his lips. He pressed the valves up and down. Louis wasn't sure how to use them, but he knew he could figure it out.

Louis blew. The sound that came out of the horn surprised him. It was clear and bright, loud and warm at the same time.

"Wow!" said Louis.

"Keep playing!" Alex said. "Show the man what you can do."

Louis began to play, getting the hang of the valves as he went along. He played "Home Sweet Home" to start. Then he played a fast tune, "Salty Dog."

The pawnshop man's foot began tapping. He smiled. "That kid is good," he told Alex.

"Sure he is! That's why we're looking for a real horn for him. He's been blowing on a tin horn long enough. If he had a real horn, he'd be good enough to play with King Oliver."

"Maybe I can help him," the pawnshop man said. "I'll let the boy have that horn for fifteen dollars."

"That's real kind of you, but fifteen dollars is still more than we can pay," Alex told him. He turned to Louis. "Give the man his horn. We need to get back to the junkyard."

It broke Louis's heart to hand over that beautiful horn. But he had no choice. He didn't have fifteen dollars. Even if he had, he couldn't spend that much money on himself when his family needed so many things. Louis's shoulders slumped as he headed for the door.

"Wait a minute," the pawnshop man said. "That kid sure can play. I agree with you. He needs a real horn. I'd like to help him out. How much money do you have?"

Louis was about to say a dollar when he felt Alex's elbow jab him in the arm. Louis knew what that meant. It meant *be quiet and let me do the talking*.

"Not much," Alex said. "Maybe we could go as high as five bucks. I know you don't have a horn that cheap. Thanks for letting us look. And thanks for letting Louis try out that trumpet."

Alex turned to open the door.

"Hold on," the pawnshop man said. "Let me see what I can do."

Louis and Alex waited while the man went into the back room. They heard rattling and scraping as the man moved boxes and barrels. At last, he found what he was looking for.

"How about this?" the man said. "It's a B-flat cornet." He put a battered horn on the counter in front of Louis. The horn was so old the brass had turned green. There were spiderwebs in the bell. The valves squeaked when Louis pressed them. The poor old horn was scratched and dented from one end to the other. It looked like it had been thrown in the trash.

Alex looked at Louis. "What do you think?"

Louis shook his head. He didn't want this horn. It was just a piece of junk. It belonged in the back of the junk wagon with the bottles and tin cans.

"Thanks, mister," Louis told the man. "I'll keep looking."

"Wait just a minute," the pawnshop man said. "I know what you're thinking. You think that if a horn looks like a piece of junk, that's what it must be. You're wrong. I've been in business thirty years. I've seen all kinds of people come in here with all kinds of horns—trumpets, cornets, tubas, saxophones. What a horn looks like doesn't matter. You can polish the brass. You can oil the valves. You can dust the cobwebs. All that counts is the sound that comes out. Give the horn a chance. Hear how it plays before you make up your mind."

"He's right, Louis," said Alex. "Give the horn a chance. What do we have to lose? Maybe you'll like it."

The pawnshop man wiped off the dust and cob-webs with his handker-chief. He squirted oil into the valves and moved them up and down until they stopped squeaking. He took off the old mouthpiece and put a clean one on it. Then he handed the cornet to Louis.

Louis began to play. He started with "After the Ball." Then he switched to "The Saints,"

the most famous song in New Orleans.

Oh, when the saints go marching in.
Oh, when the saints go marching in.

The old horn played beautifully! Louis could slide from one note to another without any trouble at all. It was as if he and the old cornet were singing together.

Oh Lord, I want to be in that number
When the saints go marching in.

"What did I tell you?" the pawnshop man told Alex. "Don't go by looks. That kid and that horn were made for each other. Give him a little time to practice on it and I wouldn't be surprised if King Oliver himself stops to listen."

King Oliver! Did the pawnshop man really think he was that good? Louis held the cornet tight. He didn't want to let go of it. It might be old and beat-up, but Louis knew he had to have this horn. He had to!

"Eight dollars and it's yours," said the pawnshop man. "I'll throw in a new mouthpiece. Only eight bucks and you take it away with you. What do you say?"

Alex glanced at Louis from the corner of his eye. Louis knew what that meant. *Don't say a word.*

Louis put the horn back on the counter. He held it for an extra moment. The blackened greenish brass felt warm to his touch. He turned to the door.

"Wait outside with Rosie," Alex said. "I'll be along in a minute."

"Goodbye, horn," Louis whispered to himself as he stepped into the street.

5

A Jar of Oil

Louis sat in the wagon, waiting for Alex to come out of the pawnshop. What was keeping him?

Louis reached for his tin horn to pass the time. Then he realized he didn't have a tin horn. He didn't have any horn at all. Louis felt blue. He felt like playing the blues.

There was magic in the blues, his mother, May Ann, always said. The blues was sad music, but it had the power to take sadness away. It was true. Whenever Louis felt bad, he always played himself some blues. The blues made him feel better.

Without his horn, Louis couldn't play the blues, but he could still sing them. He hummed slow and sad while he waited for the words to come.

Wish I had a real horn,
I'd blow it loud and strong.
Wish I had a real horn,
I'd blow it loud and strong.
I'd blow it in the daytime.
I'd blow it all night long.

"Where's Alex? What's taking him so long?" Louis said. Rosie shook her head. She didn't know, either.

Louis sang a few more verses. They made him feel a little better, but not even the blues could fix what was wrong. Louis needed a real horn. How could he go back to playing a tin horn after playing on a real cornet?

Rosie nodded and flicked her tail as if she understood.

Alex came out of the pawnshop. He carried a gunnysack on his back. Alex slung the sack in the back of the wagon. He climbed up to sit next to Louis.

"No horn?" Louis asked.

"No horn," said Alex. "The man's a *goniff*. A thief. He wanted eight dollars and he would not come down. Eight dollars for a beat-up piece of junk. Forget about it! Don't worry, Louis. We'll find a horn for you. And when we do, it will be a real horn. Not something that looks like it fell off the junk wagon."

"What's in the sack?" Louis asked.

"I asked the man what else he had in the back of the store," Alex explained. "Maybe he had some broken instruments or parts of instruments that were too beat-up to play. He gave me that whole sack for a dime. Let's head back to the junkyard. I want Pop to take a look. Pop can fix anything. If he can get those instruments to play, we can sell them ourselves."

Louis wondered if there were any horn pieces in that sack. Maybe Pop Karnofsky could put them together to make a horn for him. That would be better than nothing.

It only took an hour to get back to the junkyard. Alex handed Pop Karnofsky the sack from the pawnshop. He spoke to Pop in another language. The language was Yiddish. It was the language the Karnofskys spoke in Russia. The Karnofsky family lived in Russia before they came to America.

Louis did not understand what Alex and his father were saying. He did not speak Yiddish, but he knew a few words. Alex had taught him.

Shalom meant "hello."

Tsuris meant "troubles."

Mazel meant "good luck."

"I could sure use some *mazel*," Louis grumbled to himself. "Today, all I'm getting is *tsuris.*"

Not even the silver dollar in his pocket could cheer him up.

Louis helped Alex unload the wagon. Then they turned around and started back through the city streets to collect more junk.

Louis and Alex brought the wagon home at dusk. Morris unhitched Rosie and led her to her stall. Louis and Alex unloaded the junk. After they finished, they washed their hands and faces at the pump. Alex combed his hair. Louis straightened his jacket. They entered the house together.

Louis had never seen the house so brightly lit. Mama Karnofsky stood at the stove. She wore a snow-white apron. A white tablecloth covered the table. She had set out the best china plates, along with the best glasses and silverware. A brass candelabra with nine branches stood in the window. It held two unlit candles. Louis had never seen anything like it. The polished brass gleamed like the twenty-five-dollar trumpet at the pawnshop.

Mama, Pop, and Morris greeted Louis. "Happy Hanukkah! We are so glad you can celebrate Hanukkah with us."

"This looks like Christmas, but without a tree," Louis said. "Is Hanukkah some kind of Jewish Christmas?"

"People sometimes think so because the two holidays come at the same time of year," Morris explained. "Hanukkah celebrates a time long ago when a foreign king ruled the Jewish land. He would not let our people worship God in our own way. He forced us to bow down to idols. He killed anyone who refused. But a hero rose up. His name was Judah Maccabee. He drove the foreign soldiers out of our land and won back our freedom."

Alex continued. He told Louis, "Every

Hanukkah we light the *menorah*, the special candleholder that you see in the window. We light it so we will never forget the miracle that happened in those days. When Judah Maccabee entered the Holy Temple, he found

there was only enough oil to light the Great Menorah for one day. But God made a miracle. That little bit of oil lasted for eight days and eight nights."

"Then how come the menorah has branches for nine candles?" Louis asked.

"One is the servant candle," said Morris. "We use it to light the others."

"Tonight is the first night of Hanukkah, so we'll use the servant candle to light one candle," said Alex. "Tomorrow is the second night, so we light two candles and the servant candle. On the last night, we'll light eight candles, plus the servant candle. Got it?"

"I dig!" said Louis.

"You must always remember these things, Louis," said Pop Karnofsky. "Hanukkah teaches us important lessons. Never give up. Keep on trying. You never know what you can do until you try."

"That's what my mother, May Ann, always tells me," said Louis.

"Your mother must be a very wise woman. I would like to meet her someday," said Mama Karnofsky. "Now let us all gather around to light the menorah."

Pop Karnofsky lit the servant candle. He passed the candle to Louis so he could light the candle for the first night. The family joined hands with Louis and said the blessings together.

"It's time for presents," Morris said. There were presents for everyone. Alex and Morris got two colorful silk neckties.

"Don't we look like sports?" they laughed.

Mama Karnofsky got a lace handkerchief. Pop Karnofsky got a new brass watch chain for his pocket watch.

The biggest present was for Louis.

"What is it?" Louis asked.

"Open it and find out," said Alex.

Louis untied the ribbon around the box. He lifted the lid. Inside was a cornet, a bit dented in places, but shining like the menorah with the gleam of polished brass.

"Where did you get this?" Louis asked.

"Remember that beat-up old horn from the pawnshop?" said Alex. "I bargained with the man while you waited in the wagon. He let me have the horn for five dollars. When you drive

a junk wagon, you learn how to bargain!
That's what was in the sack. I wanted it to be a
surprise. A special surprise for Hanukkah. I
wanted you to have a Hanukkah present from
all of us. And it is from all of us. Morris ham-
mered out most of the dents. Pop ran hot oil
through the horn to clean it out. And Mama
polished it until it shined."

"And what a job that was! Don't ask!" Mama exclaimed.

"How does it sound? Play it, Louis! We want to hear you!" The Karnofskys spoke all at once.

But Louis couldn't play. He couldn't even speak. He felt sick to his stomach. He wanted to have a real horn of his own more than anything else in the world. But not like this. The Karnofskys felt sorry for him. They didn't believe he would ever have a real horn unless they gave it to him.

Louis remembered his mother's words. "We work hard and we get by. We always pay our own way."

"I'm sorry. I don't want this," Louis stammered. He put the cornet on the table and walked to the door.

"Louis, come back! What's wrong?" Alex called after him.

Louis didn't answer. He ran out into the night without looking back.

6

A Talk with Rosie

Louis didn't go far. He ran to the little stable at the end of the junkyard.

Rosie put her head down when she saw Louis. He scratched her behind the ears. "What am I gonna do, Rosie?" Louis asked her. "Alex spent five dollars buying that horn. Mama, Pop, and Morris must have spent all afternoon cleaning it up. I know they want me to be happy, but I can't keep it. I'd feel like a bum, like a poor old tramp standing on the corner with his hand out, begging."

Rosie nodded her head up and down, as if she understood.

"The Karnofskys are gonna be real mad at me. I don't blame them. I cost them a lot of money and made them feel bad. They'll fire me, most likely, and then I won't have a job. There goes the dollar I bring home every day. May Ann only makes fifty cents. How are we gonna live on that? Aw, Rosie! I feel like crying. I lost the best job I ever had. I don't have a tin horn. I don't have a real horn. I don't have a job. All I got is the blues."

Rosie shook her head back and forth as if to say, "Nope, you're wrong."

"Huh!" Louis snorted. "You're a horse. What do you know?"

"She knows a lot, that horse. More than you think."

Louis turned around. Pop Karnofsky stood in the stable door. Louis looked around for a place to hide.

"Don't run away, Louis," Pop said. "That's not how you solve a problem. No matter what happens, you're not going to lose your job. I promise."

Just hearing those words made Louis feel better.

"So tell me why you don't want that beautiful horn?" Pop Karnofsky continued.

"Because it's charity, Pop. Because it's begging," said Louis. "I feel poor. I feel ashamed. I need to earn the money to buy my own horn. I don't care if it takes forever. That's the only way it would ever really be mine."

Pop Karnofsky nodded. "Now I understand. Let me tell you a story, Louis. Our family left Russia with nothing. We arrived in America with no more than the clothes we wore. We didn't have jobs. We didn't have money. We couldn't even speak English. We needed help."

"Who helped you?" Louis asked.

"Some very kind people," Pop explained. "They helped us get a start in America. They loaned us money to come to New Orleans and buy the junkyard."

"They gave you money?" Louis asked. "Didn't that feel like begging?"

"No," said Pop. "It wasn't begging. It was a loan. We didn't want a gift. We were just like you. We wanted to work hard. We only needed some help. So we borrowed the money. Now we pay it back, a little every month. In a few years, the loan will be paid and the junkyard will be ours. The money we pay back is used to help other poor families. Around and around it goes. Someone helped us. We help someone else. Like you."

"I don't need any help," Louis said.

"Everybody needs help sometimes," Pop said. "The hard part is knowing how to do it right. That's where we slipped up. But we can fix that."

"I think I get it, Pop," Louis said. "That horn cost five dollars. I'll pay you back with money from my wages. Fifty cents a week until the horn is mine. It won't be charity because I'm paying for that horn myself. I only needed a little help to get started."

"It's a deal," said Pop. He and Louis shook hands. Louis took the silver dollar out of his pocket. "Here's my first payment, Pop," he said. "Now I only owe you four dollars."

"That horn will be yours before you know it," said Pop.

My own horn, thought Louis. *I have a real horn at last!*

7

Sweet Dreams

Louis returned to the Hanukkah party with Pop Karnofsky.

"Louis, I'm really sorry that we—" Alex began.

"Everything's fine," said Pop. "We solved the problem together. Louis is going to pay us back for the horn. He'll have a real horn and we'll have Louis. So let the party begin!"

Louis didn't know what to say. He couldn't find the right words. But music didn't need words. Louis knew how to say how he felt with music.

He raised the shining cornet to his lips and started playing the Hanukkah song that the family sang together.

Ma'oz tzur yeshuati,
L'cha na'eh l'shabeyach.
Tikon beyt tefilati
V'sham todah n'zabeyach. . . .

The notes poured from Louis's horn. They filled the room with the light of the candles. All the love and joy that Louis felt for the Karnofskys shined through his music. Louis had a real horn. All he wanted to do was blow.

The Karnofskys clapped their hands. "That's wonderful, Louis! Play for us some more!"

Louis did. He played the music he knew best. He played the music he loved. He played the blues from the streets and alleys of Storyville.

Louis thought about the blues as he played. The music seemed to say, "You can knock us down. You can push us back. You can make us so tired we can hardly stand. But you can never make us give up."

The blues was a lot like that

little jar of oil in the Hanukkah story. Nobody thought it could burn so long.

But it did!

What a party that was! Louis thought it was more fun than Christmas. He ate and ate. Mama Karnofsky worried that he would not

get enough. Every time Louis emptied his plate, she filled it.

Louis ate *latkes,* hot from the pan. Latkes are potato pancakes, drenched with applesauce and sour cream. He ate *blintzes.* Blintzes are rolled pancakes. Mama Karnofsky filled them with cottage cheese and raspberry jam. Louis ate them as fast as Mama Karnofsky could put them on his plate.

"Slow down, Louis. Save some for the rest of us," said Alex.

But Mama Karnofsky said, "Louis can eat as much as he wants. I want him to eat so he will grow up to be big and strong. He has to be big and strong to blow his new horn."

Everybody ate until they could eat no more. Then they cleared the table. Morris and Alex showed Louis how to play the dreidel game. The winning letter *gimel* came up every time Louis spun the little top.

* * *

Louis had a wonderful time at the Hanukkah party. He forgot to look at the clock. It was already late when he started for home.

"We'll see you tomorrow, Louis. Happy Hanukkah!" the Karnofskys said.

What a day it had been! Louis walked home through the streets of Storyville. In the morning, he had carried a tin horn in his pocket. Now he cradled a shining cornet in his arms. He had a real horn at last!

Storyville had come alive after the sun went down. The streets were filled with sports and their ladies, out for a good time. The clubs were jumping. Music was everywhere. Jazz, blues, ragtime.

Louis wanted to be part of it. He lifted his horn and blew it all the way to the door of Pete Lala's place. King Oliver was blowing up a storm. The melody flew out the door and danced around the street. Louis picked it up with his horn. He stretched it out, twirled it around, and blew it right back.

The music stopped. Louis looked up. Joe Oliver stood in front of him. He looked angry.

"Boy, was that you blowing that horn?" Joe Oliver asked.

"Uh-huh," Louis stammered. He did not know what to say. He didn't want Joe Oliver, the King of Storyville, to be angry with him.

Joe Oliver smiled. He opened his mouth and laughed long and hard. Then he held out

his hand to shake hands with Louis. "You're good, boy!" Joe Oliver said. "Keep practicing. Come see me someday. Come see me when you get real good. I'll let you play in my band."

Louis ran all the way home. Joe Oliver had shaken his hand! Joe Oliver said he was good! Joe Oliver! The King! What would May Ann and Mama Lucy say to that? He could not wait to tell them about everything that had happened to him today.

But it would have to wait for some other time. It was late. May Ann and Mama Lucy had already gone to bed. They were sound asleep. Louis did not want to wake them. But he was so excited. He had to tell somebody.

"I got a new horn. A real horn. And Joe Oliver said I was good," Louis whispered into the darkness. He got into bed and closed his eyes.

That night, Louis had wonderful dreams.
They all came true.

Author's Note

While some of the events of this story are fiction, most are based on actual episodes in the life of trumpeter Louis Armstrong (1900–1971), one of the world's greatest musicians and a key figure in the development of jazz.

In the course of his lifetime, Mr. Armstrong told several different—and contradictory—stories of how he acquired his first horn. My source for this story is an unpublished memoir written in 1969, "Louis Armstrong + the Jewish Family in New Orleans, La., the Year of 1907."

The full text of the memoir can be found in

Louis Armstrong, in His Own Words: Selected Writings (Oxford University Press, 1999), edited by Thomas Brothers.

Other recommended books about Louis Armstrong are Laurence Bergreen's *Louis Armstrong: An Extravagant Life* (Broadway Books, 1998) and Louis Armstrong's autobiography *Satchmo: My Life in New Orleans* (Da Capo Press, 1986). Also highly recommended is *Jazz: A Film by Ken Burns* (PBS Home Video, 2000).

New Orleans had several outstanding horn players. Joe Oliver wasn't acknowledged as "King" until he moved to Chicago in 1918, but Louis always regarded him as the best of the best. "Joe Oliver has always been my inspiration and my idol. No trumpet player ever had the fire that Oliver had. Man, he could really *punch* a number" (*Louis Armstrong, in His Own Words,* p. 37).

Glossary

New Orleans has always been an international city where a gumbo of languages is spoken. In certain neighborhoods, Louis would have heard French, Italian, Spanish, or German more frequently than English.

Yiddish is a language spoken by Jewish people, like the Karnofskys, whose families came from Central and Eastern Europe. Yiddish is written with Hebrew letters, although it is mostly German, with many Hebrew and Slavic words.

BAMBINO (bam-BEE-no): a little boy or baby. *Italian*

BEIGNET (ben-YAY): a sugar-dusted dough-nut popular in New Orleans. *French*

BLINTZ: a thin pancake rolled around a filling. *Yiddish*

CORNET (kor-NET): a brass instrument resembling a small trumpet. *French, English*

DREIDEL (DRAY-dul): a four-sided top marked with Hebrew letters. It is used in children's games on Hanukkah. *Yiddish*

GONIFF (GON-if): a thief. *Hebrew, Yiddish*

HANUKKAH (HAH-nuh-kah): the Jewish Festival of Lights. *Hebrew*

KAPUT (kah-PUT): dead, finished, useless. *Yiddish*

KASHA (KAH-shuh): a porridge made from buckwheat. *Yiddish*

KNAIDLACH (K'NAYD-lahkh): small dumplings, usually served in soup. (The last syllable is pronounced like the Scottish *loch*.) *Yiddish*

LATKE (LAHT-kuh): a potato pancake traditionally served at Hanukkah. *Yiddish*

LOKSHEN (LOCK-shun): egg noodles. *Yiddish*

"MA'OZ TZUR" (MAH-ohz TZUR): a centuries-old hymn sung after lighting the Hanukkah candles. (The English version of the hymn begins, "Rock of Ages, let our song / Praise Thy saving power. / Thou, amidst the raging foes, / Wast our sheltering tower.") *Hebrew*

MAZEL (MAH-zul): luck, good fortune. *Hebrew, Yiddish*

MENORAH (muh-NOR-uh): a candelabra with seven or nine branches that is used in Jewish worship. The Hanukkah menorah has nine branches. *Hebrew*

SHABBOS (SHAH-bus): the Jewish Sabbath, a day of rest. *Hebrew, Yiddish*

SHALOM (shah-LOHM): hello, goodbye, peace. *Hebrew, Yiddish*

TSURIS (TZUH-ris): misery, troubles. *Hebrew, Yiddish*

About the Author

Eric A. Kimmel grew up in Brooklyn, New York, loving the music of Louis Armstrong, who lived a few miles away in the neighboring borough of Queens. New Orleans is one of his favorite cities. To research this book, he traveled to New Orleans to track down the streets and neighborhoods that appear in the story.

Eric Kimmel is the award-winning author of several children's classics, including *Anansi and the Moss-Covered Rock* and *Hershel and the Hanukkah Goblins*. He and his wife, Doris, live in Portland, Oregon.